Start your journey into the life of freedom, power and authority rightfully yours as a child of the King… and be equipped to lead others onto this same pathway.

Jocelyn A Drozda
M.Ed, B.Ed

Stand in Freedom: A Journey into Kingdom Identity
Copyright©2025 Jocelyn Anne Drozda

All rights reserved.

Unless otherwise noted, Scripture quotations are from The ESV® Bible (The Holy Bible, English Standard Version®), copyright © 2001 by Crossway, a publishing ministry of Good News Publishers. Used by permission. All rights reserved.

Scriptures taken from the Holy Bible, New International Version®, NIV®. Copyright © 1973, 1978, 1984, 2011 by Biblica, Inc.™ Used by permission of Zondervan. All rights reserved worldwide. www.zondervan.com The "NIV" and "New International Version" are trademarks registered in the United States Patent and Trademark Office by Biblica, Inc.™

Scripture taken from the New King James Version®. Copyright © 1982 by Thomas Nelson. Used by permission. All rights reserved.

ISBN# 978-1-998532-40-7

Published in the United States of America
Printed in the United States of America
www.aheliapublishing.org

AHELIA
PUBLISHING, LLC
Augusta, Montana

Soul Healing
STAND IN FREEDOM
A JOURNEY INTO KINGDOM IDENTITY

Jocelyn A Drozda
jdrozda@myaccess.ca
Ascend Seminars
www.ascend-seminars.com

TABLE OF CONTENTS

Dedication 6
Introduction 7

**Part One - The Wisdom of the Body:
Unlocking Trauma from Within 9**
Definitions 10
Introduction 11
Trauma Defined 12
The Origins of Trauma 12
The Symptoms of Trauma 15
The Triggers and Roots of Trauma 16
Trauma Inducing Events 18
The Mind's Response 19
The Spiritual Attack Within 22
Resolving Trauma 24

Part Two - Three Part Beings 29
Three Part Beings 31
Pryer - Declaring Ownership and Purpose .. 34

Part Three - Red Flags 35
Red Flags/Sign Posts 37
Red Flags (Worksheet) 38
The S.O.S. of Pain 39
Prayer Releasing Shame, Guilt and
    Condemnation 40
Coping Mechanisms 41
Prayer for Repentance 42
Protective Behaviours 43
Prayer to Release Protective Behaviours 44

Part Four - Kingdom Identity 45
Kingdom Identity 47
The Fruit of Kingdom Identity 47
False Identities: Labels and
    Lies of the enemy 48
Demarkations of enemy Traps and Snares .. 49
The Creative Power of Words 50
The Function of Words 51
Prayer for Repentance 53
Untangling the Web of Deceit:
    Deciphering Labels and Lies 54
Responding 55
Dismantling enemy Labels and Lies 57

Part Five - Connecting with Trauma 59
Connecting with Trauma
    Processing Sheet 61

Part Six - Staying Free 69
Walk in Rest and Peace 71
Practice Gratitude 71
Serve 72
Fast 72
Fellowship 73
Live Holy 73
Obedience and Surrender 74
Keep Seeking Your Healing 75
Be the Gold Refine in the Fire 75

Endnotes 77

Appendices 79

Appendix 1 - Symptoms of Trauma 81

Appendix 2 - Case Studies 82

Appendix 3 - Enemy Lies, Spirit
    Families and Holy Spirit Infilling 84

Appendix 4 - Spiritual Strongmen 91

Appendix 5 - Our Identity in Christ
    Scriptures 97

Note Pages 100

DEDICATION

Dedicated to those who have set their face as flint, determined to live a life of freedom and fullness, wholeness, righteousness, joy and peace; those determined to walk in the character and nature of Christ Almighty, stopping at nothing to bare His image and be a vessel fit for His service.

THE JOURNEY:

"His eyes were running to and fro ... who will dare to prepare?

Who will step out onto the water? Who will wait for My timing?

Who will lean in to hear? Who will not stop until every hidden

thing has been opened and every hidden scar is shown to Me,

that I may make this one whole, a vessel fit for My use?

Ahhh ... I see this one!

This one is perfect!"

(Prophetic word by Pastor C. Nightingale - adapted)

"He is wooing you from the jaws of distress to a spacious place free from restriction, to the comfort of your table laden with choice food."
Job 36:16 NIV

"... a man of his standing..."
It is a phrase used to describe a person who commands respect or admiration due to their reputation, rank, or influence. (ludwig.guru.com)

STAND IN FREEDOM
Introduction

Once we know our **Kingdom Identity,** we stand in freedom. We stand in the authority and position granted us as heirs with Jesus. We stand in the power afforded us as a child of the King. However, the journey to arrive at this knowledge and understanding can be painful. And we have learned to avoid pain at all cost. Yet pain is purposeful. It is a warning, like an SOS, placed in our body or soul. It forces us to finally take notice that something is out of alignment, and requires us to look beneath the surface to bring about the healing of our soul, which leads to freedom, authority and power.

This pain is not a call to self-medicate with distraction to curb those red flags screaming their SOS. We need to stop masking the symptoms and start healing the internal wounds at their source. This is how the pain is released and we come into alignment with our Kingdom Identity: knowing and fully believing we are who God says we are, and He is who He says He is.

Walking through your deep, personal pain is a hard journey—but no harder than a life filled with depression, anxiety, bitterness, jealousy, addiction, broken relationships, turmoil, chaos and sorrow…

Your choice is therefore not between pain and no pain, but between intentional, intense pain for a shorter time as you walk out your healing into a life of freedom, or the long term pain of continual dysfunction. As a child of Christ, the choice is clear. God is calling us to arise and impact the world around us. Will you make the wise choice?

Prayer:

STAND IN FREEDOM
Part One

THE WISDOM OF THE BODY

UNLOCKING TRAUMA FROM WITHIN

Definitions:

Agency - having say in one's own life.

Dissociation - disconnection from oneself and the outside world.

Kingdom identity - we are who God says we are. God is who He says He is. If it is not in the Word of God, it is not who we were created to be.

Personality - the enduring characteristics and behaviour that comprise a person's unique adjustment to life, including major traits, interests, drives, values, self-concept, abilities, and emotional patterns. (apa.org)

Physiology - the functioning of the body.

Psychosomatic - considers the interaction between the soul (mind, will, emotions) and the body; how the mind/will/emotions affect the body.

Soma/Somatic - referring to or affecting the *body*, with a distinction from the *mind*.

Soul - consisting of the *mind (reason)*, *will* (choose) and *emotions (feel)*.

Trauma - the emotional, physical and psychological **RESPONSE** in an organism to a shocking, disturbing, or intensely stressful event or series of events.

Visceral - comes from or is felt in the deep, internal organs of the body—the gut rather than the brain.

Introduction

PEOPLE TELL YOU TO LEAVE THE PAST BEHIND. BUT WHAT IF ITS physical, emotional, psychological, and spiritual aftermath won't leave you behind? The body is wise. God created it with the wisdom it needs to survive—to guard the sanctity of life at all costs. It locks away the things trying to harm it—then screams at the tops of its lungs for rescue.

Many people are impacted by trauma they don't even know is there—not recognizing that some of the pervasive negative issues in their lives are directly related. Trauma imprints on the body and soul, expressed as present physical reactions. It needs to be voiced. It needs to be confronted. It needs to be renegotiated, reframed.

It is time to sever the tentacles of trauma and its far-reaching impact. Once you have deeper understanding of the inner and outer workings of trauma, it is easier to "connect the dots" in your own life and in those around you, enabling you to recognize its manifestations, and thus able to tackle them head on.

Trauma Defined

Trauma IS THE EMOTIONAL, PHYSICAL AND PSYCHOLOGICAL **RESPONSE** in an organism to a shocking, disturbing, or intensely stressful event or series of events. The impact of unresolved trauma can have long-lasting negative repercussions on the mental, physical, emotional, social and spiritual well-being of an individual.

SHOCK TRAUMA is considered one specific, severe event.

DEVELOPMENTAL TRAUMA refers to ongoing negative circumstances or events, including those of *commission*, such as child abuse, and *omission*, such as neglect. It is imperative to note that the neglect aspect, where a child does not sufficiently attach to their caregiver, can have as significant an impact as outward abuse.

The Origin of Trauma

AS YOU ENCOUNTER A THREATENING (OR PERCEIVED AS SUCH) situation, your body prepares for its defence against the attack. The brain activates the nervous system, signalling the glands to produce *adrenaline* and *cortisol*, hormones that will cause almost immediate physiological changes.

The heart beats faster to supply more blood into needed areas. The breathing rate increases to send more oxygen to the brain, increasing alertness of the senses. Blood sugars are released to provide immediate access to more energy.

All of these functions work together to increase the body's chances of survival, giving it what it needs to FIGHT or to run away (FLIGHT) from the danger. It all happens in micro-seconds, at an unconscious level.

However, when the brain perceives it is not possible to escape from the threat, it becomes overwhelmed and sends the body into an immobility response—a literal FREEZING—which in itself, can also function to evade death in certain situations. This condition provides a numbing from pain as well, if it is the time of demise for the organism.

As the person or animal takes action for its protection (fight or flight), it expends this surplus of energy. Once the danger is passed and the energy is spent, the body returns to normal function. With the response to the threat being COMPLETED and RESOLVED—the danger was successfully evaded, averted, overcome—NO TRAUMATIZATION OCCURS.

If this energy is not released, as is the case with the FREEZE response, it becomes LOCKED IN THE NERVOUS SYSTEM. With nothing to signal the conclusion of the danger, the body remains in the hypervigilant state, from the muscles right down to the cells, continually searching and ON GUARD for the now non-existent threat. It creates a perpetual cycle. When you are looking for something that doesn't exist, it is impossible to resolve. So you keep looking…

In his book, *The Body Keeps the Score*, Dr. Bessel van der Kolk notes: "As long as the trauma is not resolved, the stress hormones that the body secretes to protect itself keep circulating, and the defensive movements and emotional responses keep getting replayed."[1]

In an attempt to manage or contain the excess energy in the heightened nervous system, the body develops the "symptoms of trauma." Dr. van der

Kolk refers to this as "suppressing inner chaos" as the body "attempts to maintain control over unbearable physiological reactions..."[2]

Our nervous system is physically altered after trauma. Symptoms can be minimal or severe. They may appear shortly after the original traumatic event, or build up over time. This makes it harder to connect the new symptoms with the former trauma response.

An overreactive response to a minor incident can indicate a previous, more serious trauma event had occurred and left its mark. (Much like bumping your arm would not hurt very much—unless it is already bleeding, broken and bruised!) In his work with trauma, Dr Peter Levine described the onset of traumatic symptoms as being like both the gas and the brake pedal of a vehicle being simultaneously pressed:[3]

"... the inner racing of the nervous system (engine) and the outer immobility (brake) of the body creates a forceful turbulence inside the body similar to a tornado. This tornado of energy is the focal point out of which form the symptoms of traumatic stress."

STAND IN FREEDOM — Reflective Activity

AS YOU THINK ABOUT THE FULL FORCE OF TRAUMA AS NOTED BY THE ABOVE QUOTE, WHAT HAS BEEN ITS NEGATIVE IMPACT ON YOU OR YOUR LOVED ONES?

The Symptoms of Trauma

THE SYMPTOMS OF TRAUMA ARE DIVERSE AND EXTENSIVE. THEY increase as the frozen energy accumulates. The list of symptoms may include:

Anxiety	Digestive issues	Neck pain
Anorexia	Disease	Nightmares
Amnesia	Dissociation	Panic attacks
Avoidance	Endocrine problems	Phobias
Asthma	Fibromyalgia	Promiscuity
Blindness	Flashbacks	Rage
Back pain	Immune Issues	Shame
Chronic fatigue	Inflammation	Temper tantrums
Deafness	Insomnia	Trembling
Denial	Migraines	Victim mentality
Depression		

[See Appendix 1 for more extensive listing]

STAND IN FREEDOM
Reflective Activity

READ THROUGH THE LIST OF SYMPTOMS. HIGHLIGHT ANY WHICH YOU OR SOMEONE YOU KNOW HAS SIGNIFICANTLY EXPERIENCED.

The Triggers and Roots of Trauma

ALMOST ANY HAPPENING, SIGHT, SOUND, SMELL, TASTE OR BODILY sensation can trigger a traumatic response in a person who has previously been traumatized. These TRIGGERS can throw a person right back into the depths of their physiological and emotional trauma response as the memory is activated. To their minds and bodies, the trauma is taking place *right at that very moment* instead of in the past. There is no differentiation.

These triggers, usually minor, are not the root of the original trauma. Bear in mind, though, that even seemingly benign events can invoke a traumatic response, especially in infants and young children who lack the ability to navigate a threatening situation. It is in childhood that much of our traumatization has already occurred and remains unhealed in the body and mind, ready to be reactivated again and again.

Being left alone in a room, briefly losing sight of a parent, storms, scary movies, shocking events on the screen, insects in unexpected places, nightmares, losing precious objects—any situation in which you feel loss, alone, bitter, angry, rejected, hurt, defeated, hopeless, etc., can be the source of an original trauma wound, or a situation of re-traumatization.

ESSENTIALLY, TRAUMA CAN BE THE RESULT OF ANYTHING CAUSING THAT SHARP INTAKE OF BREATH AND RESULTING RUSH OF ADRENALINE.

The body, through the senses, triggers the soul (mind, will and emotions) and the soul triggers the body, causing a perpetual cycle.

STAND IN FREEDOM
Group Activity

RECORD THE EVENTS WHICH YOU BELIEVE WILL CAUSE AN ORIGINAL TRAUMA WOUND. (SHARE. MARK OFF ANY READ BY OTHER GROUPS.)

Trauma inducing Events

Major events that can create a traumatic response in people as outlined by Levine include:[4]

- Abandonment
- Abuse - emotional, physical, sexual
- Accidents/Falls
- Anesthesia
- Attacks of violence
- Betrayal
- Bullying
- Difficult births
- Exposure to threats against others
- Exposure to violence, danger, death or injury
- Illness
- Intra-uterine events
- Mother's stress during gestation
- Natural disasters
- Neglect
- Prolonged immobilizations (castings, forced restraint)
- Rape
- Rejection
- Sudden loss (death, divorce, moving)
- Surgical and medical procedures
- Terrorism/War

At times, our bodies may register an event as trauma-inducing, right down to the cellular level, even though our brains understand its benefit. As Levine[5] illustrates:

"Even though a person may recognize that an operation is necessary, and despite the fact that they are unconscious as the surgeon cuts through flesh, muscle, and bone, it still registers in the body as a life-threatening event."

The Mind's Response

THE CLASH BETWEEN THE *SELF PRESERVATION* AT THE CORE OF OUR beings and an event BEYOND ENDURABILITY causes a fracture of self—a split between body and soul. This disconnection can go deeper—splitting the very parts of the *soul* itself. (*Feeling* from rational *thought* — *emotion* from *mind*).

Our mind stuffs the part of ourselves who suffered the event, all of its sensations, all of its memories, all of its emotions, into a tiny compartment of its own and locks it away. With that part of us, of our lives, sealed away in the hidden recesses of our mind, either forgotten or intentionally buried, the rest of us attempts to move on.

Denial of the trauma and remaining NUMB and DISCONNECTED within ourselves and from the world around us can become a survival strategy to keep that part concealed. This serves to MAKE THE INTOLERABLE SOMEWHAT TOLERABLE, but prevents us from living life in the fullness God has intended. It robs peace, hope, and joy from our existence. Choices then consciously or subconsciously align with this state, leading to such things as substance abuse and other numbing behaviours. The numbing can be physical as well as mental and emotional:

"Disconnection between body and soul is one of the most important effects of trauma. Loss of skin sensation is a common physical manifestation of the numbness and disconnection people experience after trauma."[6]

The opposite phenomenon can also occur—everything is filtered through the lens of trauma. We can begin to hyper-consciously (or subconsciously if the memory is buried) avoid all situations which may lead to a reoccurrence. This can become a limiting factor in our lifestyles. (Fear of driving, of water, or of leaving our homes …)

Distraction strategies have a different approach yet the same impact—keeping us from any reminder of the instigating traumatic event. We develop a deep fascination and obsession with things far from the memory.

We become so occupied with anything or everything but ... ensuring our hearts will not dwell on or give any regard whatsoever, to what once was. Creating chaos/drama, seeking constant change for the sake of change, addictions, and the overindulgence in hobbies or passions are common.

All of these and other such survival strategies become a double-edged sword. They do allow us to continue with life, but one much limited or exploding with chaos. And moreover, they inhibit us from exploring and processing our response to the traumatic event—which is needed to bring true healing and freedom.

The choices we make in alignment with these survival strategies and the resulting patterns of behaviours become so deeply etched within our brains that we mistakenly believe they are a part of who we are—our *character*, our *personality*, our very *identity*—when in reality, they are an EXPRESSION OF TRAUMA.

What we believe to be character, personality, identity—has instead been shaped, altered, modified—CREATED BY TRAUMA—NOT who we were originally designed to be. It becomes our *false identity*. We can know it is false if it does not line up with our KINGDOM IDENTITY: We are who God says we are. God is who He says He is. If it is not in the Word of God, it is not who we were created to be, even if it appears to be true according to present circumstances. People indignantly cry out: "That's just who I am! That's just the way I am!" Maybe ... but it not who they were originally created to be.

Many instances of the modern psychiatric disorders may, in fact, be expressions or symptoms of trauma in disguise: depression, oppositional defiance disorder, anxiety, reactive attachment disorder, ADHD, PTSD, bipolar disorder, intermittent explosive disorder, narcissism, etc.

Levine[7] demonstrates how this concept unfolds in the development of a "victim mentality:"

"All humans who are repeatedly overwhelmed become identified with states of anxiety and helplessness. In addition, they bring this helplessness to many other situations that are perceived as threats. They make the 'decision' that they are helpless, and continue in many varied ways to prove this victimization to themselves and others. This gives in to the helpless feelings even in situations that they have the resources to master."

[See Appendix 2 for a more extensive explanation on how this occurs.]

STAND IN FREEDOM — Group Activity

READ THE CASE STUDY IN APPENDIX 2 AND ANSWER THE QUESTIONS.

The Spiritual Attack Within

During the upheaval of our entire being at the moments of trauma and its aftermath, the enemy takes this opportune moment to plant the seed of a lie in our soul. These lies form the framework for this distortion of character, personality, and identity. As these lies attack our hope, our joy, our peace, our security, our position, our relationships, our honour, our worth, our value—who we are—and who God is, they are fundamental in the formation of the *false identity*. Determined to bring destruction, these lies can threaten our very existence.

These lies tell us, "No one cares about me. It is hopeless. I am alone. I am not enough. I am dirty. I am worthless. No one loves me. I am not safe. I cannot trust God. They'd be better off without me. I'd be better off dead."

Right from the Garden of Eden with his query, "Did God really say…" the use of DECEIT is the source of the enemy's power. As we AGREE WITH THE LIES, the spiritual doors are opened, giving power to the enemy to construct situations that reinforce the lie time and again.

In effort to keep our heart safe and to never again feel that depth of pain, we make vows, essentially locking in the lies and giving them authority over our lives, as our decisions begin to align with the vows of our soul: "People will only hurt me. I will not let anyone close to me ever again!"

We are saved through faith, which comes by believing in our hearts and confessing with our mouths (Romans 10:9). As we think in our hearts, so we are (Proverbs 23:7). These verses illustrate the power of belief and confession. As we speak the lies and profess the vows made in response to trauma over our lives, they are being sealed in our souls. They are played out in our *mind*, in our *emotion*, and in our *body*, and they corrupt our *will*.

The Bible tells us that the LORD has not given us a spirit of fear, but of love, power, and a sound mind (2 Timothy 1:7). The enemy, on the other hand, capitalizes on the moment we open the spiritual door as we agree with his lies, and sends in the spirit of fear, shame, hate, lust … whatever has been given life and allowed in by the confession of our mouths and the beliefs in our heart. And now, with the physiological chaos of trauma in the body, the lies plaguing our mind, the vows influencing our decisions, and the power of the spiritual forces wreaking havoc in our emotions and relationships, the spiritual attack entwined in trauma is all encompassing; its impact—devastating.

This makes it imperative that the saints are equipped to break the bonds of trauma, setting the captives free—whether it be ourselves, those the Lord has placed in our lives, or the ones destined to be healed under our ministries.

STAND IN FREEDOM
Reflective Activity

ARE YOU RECOGNIZING ANY ASPECTS OF WHAT YOU BELIEVED TO BE YOUR CHARACTER AS PART OF A FALSE OR DISTORTED IDENTITY?

Resolving Trauma

THERE IS AN ILLUSION OF SAFETY HELD WITHIN THE SUPPRESSION OF A trauma-laden memory. As long as it is buried deep beneath our conscious mind, the associated emotions are seemingly held at bay. (Though much tumult is "coming out sideways"—only we don't recognize it as such.)

When the original wound is threatened with exposure and the memory and its flood of overwhelming negative emotions comes roaring to the forefront of our minds, PANIC and TERROR take over. They cause us to bury it even deeper, refusing to allow the exploration that will assuredly bring back the pain and the shame of the event, not to mention the physiological responses. Not surprisingly, that unearthing and exposure, done correctly, is exactly what is needed to also bring about its healing.

Van der Kolk[8] includes within his recommendations when dealing with trauma, a top down approach:

Talking, (re-)connecting with others, and allowing ourselves to know and understand what is going on with us, while processing the memories of the trauma.

And a bottom up method:

Allowing the body to have experiences that deeply and viscerally contradict the helplessness, rage, or collapse that result from trauma.

Thus, understanding the impacts of trauma—what is going on in our body and soul—is essential in beginning to understand how to process it; and doing so from a place of deep security.

To process trauma, we need:

1) A desire and determination to become whole and live out the Lord's calling for our lives. Levine acknowledges the shortfalls of secular counselling: "I must confess that the miracles of healing I have seen make some higher form of wisdom and order hard to deny."[9]

2) Courage to keep walking—even when it is painful.

3) To feel safe. Van Der Kolk recognizes, "You need a guide who is not afraid of your terror and who can contain your darkest rage, someone who can safeguard the wholeness of you while you explore the fragmented experiences that you had to keep secret for so long. Most traumatized individuals need an anchor and a great deal of coaching to do this work."[10] Who better an anchor than our triune God: God the Father, Jesus the Son, and the Holy Spirit? What a team! When we invite them into our place of trauma, everything changes.

4) To be seen, heard, validated. We need to know *"We matter."* Naming the trauma brings it out of the shadows and helps us to step out of isolation and into the community and support team that helps bring healing.

5) To IDENTIFY and RENEGOTIATE the original trauma. (Working through its impact and bringing its resolution. Details are not always necessary.

   a) To know the truth of the situation. (Child perspective verses adult; replace lie that was sown at the time of trauma with God's truth.)

   b) Cancel the vows of self-protection. (Change our language/confession.)

   c) To ask God where He was during the event; (Know that because of Him, we are not helpless.)

d) To understand and know our KINGDOM IDENTITY. (Who we are in Christ. Who God is.)

e) To forgive and release from judgment all those involved. (This does NOT mean what they did was acceptable. This does NOT mean they need to be trusted or you need to stay in relationship with them. It DOES mean the debt you feel they owe you is cancelled.)

f) To forgive and release ourself from judgment. ("You did the best you could with what you had at the time. But now you have more.")

g) To release judgments we are holding against God.

> **WHEN YOU HOLD UNFORGIVENESS AGAINST SOMEONE, EVEN AGAINST YOURSELF OR GOD, YOU ARE LOCKING YOURSELF INTO THE IDENTITY OF PERPETUAL VICTIM.**

h) To repent and renounce any of our actions and behaviours out of alignment with our identity in Christ.

i) To break any ungodly spiritual agreements, covenants, and contracts.

j) To be willing to let go of the distorted personalities and the ways in which they served you. (Victim mentality is a crucial one.)

6) Reconnection with our soul, (mind, will, emotions) our body and the world around us. (Journal. Remain present in the moment. Acknowledge our emotions as a "signpost, not a rudder.")

7) To release the undischarged energy: somatic exercises, deep tissue massage, fasting. Reconnecting with our bodies allows them to experience any sensations instead of shutting them or the process down at the first signs of physical response, and increasing the window of

tolerance for these sensations. Becoming aware of where in our body we are feeling the sensations—current sensations and pervasive symptoms helps us to process them and bring them to a conclusion. The body needs to return to a state of safety, with the ability to rest and relax. The chronic muscle tension needs to be released. Make friends with your body and acknowledge its wisdom for doing what it had to do to help you survive and keep you safe.

8) Support, community, quietness, peace, nature, enjoyment.

9) To surrender to God and trust His plan for our lives. Repentance for not trusting Him with our lives is often a part of the realignment process.

10) Be willing to face old and new challenges, reorganizing the mind and rewiring the brain.

11) To restore our ability to make choices—understanding that once you know the truth and the spiritual forces are released, you have the ability to choose differently. Automatic trauma response now becomes conscious choice. You see things differently; you have a new lens through with to see each situation. We need to restore the belief that we have *agency* — a say in our own lives.

12) To take back our God-given authority.

13) To think through the original event and predetermine a defensive strategy. Van der Kolk states: "Being able to move and *do* something to protect oneself is a critical factor in determining whether or not a horrible experience will leave long-lasting scars."[11] But, we also need to speak into our lives that Christ will guard our heart (Phil 4:7) so we (our bodies and minds) can drop their guard (hypervigilance).

STAND IN FREEDOM
Part Two

THREE PART BEINGS

Three-Part Beings

Human Beings are comprised of three parts: spirit, soul, and body.

1. **Spirit** - the place where God as Spirit dwells.

The human spirit is partitioned into three functions: CONSCIENCE, FELLOWSHIP and INTUITION.

> <u>CONSCIENCE</u> - knowing right from wrong; that place in our intellect that oscillates between our intellect (natural knowledge) and revelation. It is the "relationship between how we think and how we choose to behave."[13]
>
> <u>FELLOWSHIP</u> - Allows us to connect and commune with God and others at an intimate level.
>
> God is spirit, and those who worship him must worship in spirit and truth.
> **John 4:24**
>
> For God is my witness, whom I serve with my spirit in the gospel of his Son, that without ceasing I mention you...
> **Romans 1:9**
>
> <u>INTUITION</u> - The intuition senses the spiritual world around us. It can give us a sense of foreboding or unease as a warning when there is nothing substantial on which to base it. It is where God provides knowledge of the happenings of the unseen.
>
> When the Spirit of truth comes, he will guide you into all truth, for he will not speak on his own authority, but whatever he hears he will speak, and he will declare to you the things that are to come.
> **John 16:13**

2. **Soul**- the place where "self" dwells.

The soul is also formed by three parts: your *mind*, your *will*, and your *emotions*. It formulates your personality—who you are.[14&15]

> <u>MIND</u> - The functions of the MIND include: knowing, remembering, considering, wondering, thinking, reasoning.
>
> … for wisdom will come into your heart,
> and knowledge will be pleasant to your soul;
> **Proverbs 2:10**
>
> <u>WILL</u> - The functions of the WILL include: choosing, refusing, deciding.
>
> So that my soul chooses …
> **Job 7:15 NKJV**
>
> Now set your heart and your soul to
> seek the Lord your God.
> **1 Chronicles 22:19**
>
> <u>EMOTIONS</u> - Feeling EMOTIONS is a function of the soul. However, the will can override the emotions. *Emotions are a flag, not a rudder.*
>
> ### Hating/loathing/despising:
>
> … (the lame and the blind, *who are* hated by David's soul),…
> **2 Samuel 5:8**
>
> Their soul abhorred all manner of food…
> **Psalm 107:18**
>
> ### Joy:
>
> I will greatly rejoice in the LORD;
> **Isaiah 61:10**
>
> Gladden the soul of your servant…
> **Psalm 86:4**
>
> ### Bitterness, Misery, Grief:
>
> …all the people were bitter in soul…
> **1 Samuel 30:6**
>
> Was not my soul grieved for the needy?
> **Job 30:25**

3. **Body** - the place the physical senses dwell.

Our body uses our five senses to tangibly experience the physical world around us. Trauma is physically stored in the body—your body holds its memory, its anticipation.[16]

Aspects of which to be aware: Posture, holding muscles in tension, clenching, physical symptoms, physical pain, disease, countenance. "Constantly waiting for the other shoe to drop."

STAND IN FREEDOM — Reflective Activity

DO A QUICK INVENTORY OF YOUR BODY. ARE YOU HOLDING TENSION IN ANY MUSCLES GROUPS? CAN YOU DROP YOUR SHOULDERS FROM WHERE THEY ARE RIGHT NOW? ARE YOU CLENCHING YOUR TEETH? HOLDING YOUR BREATH? WHERE IN YOUR BODY ARE YOU STORING TRAUMA?

Declaring Ownership and Purpose

Prayer:

Jesus, You are the Way, the Truth, and the Life. All things were created through You and for You. You hold it all together. You were conceived by the Holy Spirit, born of the Virgin Mary, and are the only mediator between God and man. Through You, we have been reconciled to the Father.

You are the hope of glory. Thank You for the cross where You gave Your life as a ransom for many. Through Your shed blood, death, and resurrection, You broke the power of sin and death. You disarmed the powers and authorities, making a public spectacle of them, triumphing over them by the cross. Now, seated at the right hand of God, Your name is the one Name through which we can be saved.

I have sinned and fallen short of the glory of God; and the wages of sin is death. But Your sacrificial death and the shedding of Your blood covers sin once and for all. By accepting Your sacrifice, which I do now, I am a blood-bought child of the King of kings, restored in authority to reign with You, my sins now forgiven and washed clean.

Please open my mind and my heart to hear Your words, learn Your ways, and be obedient in walking in them. Let me hear Your heart for me, for others. I lay down my life in surrender. I trust the path You have for me. You are infinitely wise and good, and know the best way for me and for my loved ones. Be the Lord of my life. Fill me afresh with the Baptism of Your Holy Spirit. Lead me, guide me—I surrender all. In Jesus' name. Amen.

STAND IN FREEDOM
Part Three

RED FLAGS

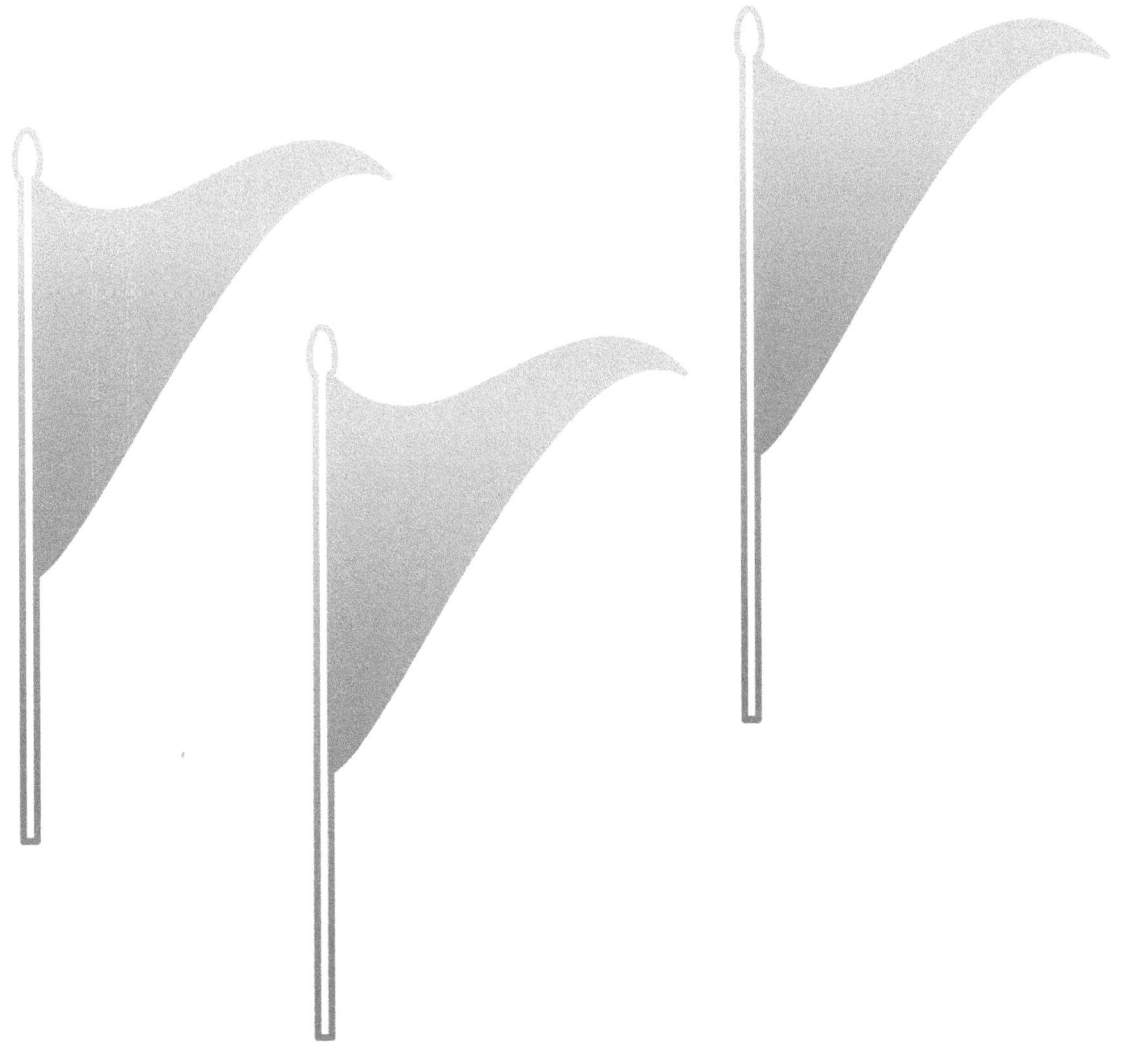

Red Flags/Sign Posts

RED FLAGS or SIGN POSTS ARE WARNINGS DESIGNED TO "CAPTURE our attention." They are an indication of a deep wound of trauma hidden beneath the surface. They can manifest through many different pathways:

Actions	Lies/False Beliefs
Anxiety	Negative Emotions
Behaviours	Obsessive thoughts
Choices	Overwhelming Emotions
Coping Mechanisms	Repeated Memories
Depression	Shut Down Emotions
Dreams	Words/Phrases
Heaviness	_____
_____	_____

STAND IN FREEDOM
Reflective Activity

HIGHLIGHT THE PATHWAYS YOU RECOGNIZE AS MANIFESTING IN YOUR LIFE OR THAT OF YOUR LOVED ONES. ON THE FOLLOWING PAGE RECORD THE SPECIFICS.

Red Flags
WHAT ARE THE RED FLAGS BLARING S.O.S. IN YOUR LIFE?

A JOURNEY INTO KINGDOM IDENTITY

THE SOS OF PAIN

TRAUMA

[SECONDARY TRAUMA]

PAIN

AVOIDANCE/ SUPPRESSION

BELIEVE LIES
(FALSE BELIEFS ABOUT GOD, SELF, OTHERS)

MAKE VOWS OF SELF PRESERVATION
["I WILL ALWAYS..."
"I WILL NEVER..."]

SHUT DOWN EMOTIONS/ EMERGENCE OF PROTECTIVE PERSONALITIES

KINGDOM IDENTITY* REPLACED BY FALSE IDENTITY
[*YOU ARE WHO GOD SAYS YOU ARE
GOD IS WHO HE SAYS HE IS]

LOCKS YOU INTO WRONG THOUGHT PATTERNS/MIND SETS
STEALS DESTINY

THE EXPRESSIONS OF PAIN BECOME YOUR CHOICES/ACTIONS/BEHAVIORS

DESTRUCTION OF SELF/OTHERS

SHAME/GUILT/ CONDEMNATION
[OVERWHELMING EMOTIONS]

Releasing Shame, Guilt & Condemnation

Prayer

Heavenly Father,

Thank you that You hear my cry. Thank you that You will never abandon me nor forsake me. I ask You now to help me get to the trauma at the root of my unhealthy attitudes, beliefs and behaviours so I can receive Your healing. I ask for Your grace and mercy to be poured out on me and those around me. Give me eyes to see, ears to hear, and a heart to understand.

Guilt, shame and condemnation, I expose you and your attempt to persuade me into keeping things hidden. I step out of partnership with you. I bring everything into the light. I walk in the light. I allow Holy Spirit access to every part of my heart—every chamber, every event, every doorway, every secret room. I remove the veil from my eyes, and I lift my face up to the Lord. I lock eyes with Jesus, and I receive His mercy, His grace and His forgiveness that comes from His blood shed on the cross for my sin, and the power that comes from His resurrection. I receive the absolution from guilt, shame, and condemnation. Every spirit of guilt, shame and condemnation, I cast you out in the name of Jesus. Out now! (Exhale deeply.)

Coping Mechanisms

OUR EXPRESSIONS OF PAIN FROM ORIGINAL OR SECONDARY TRAUMA become our choices. Our choices lead to actions. Repeated actions become behaviours—often destructive to ourselves or others. They masquerade as "coping mechanisms." If they do not have overtly negative repercussions in themselves, they still work to prevent us from dealing with the original pain.

It is important to work through these areas. But dealing with them in and of themselves will not bring complete healing. You still need to dig deeper to the original source of the pain that led you into that behaviour.

[Note any you have had issues with any time in your life.]

- Alcohol abuse
- Busyness
- Creating chaos
- Cutting
- Drugs
- Excessive risk taking
- Gambling
- Hoarding
- Inappropriate sex/Masturbation
- Overeating
- Physical gratification
- Prescription drug abuse
- Pornography
- Self harm
- Shopping/Excessive spending
- Smoking
- Speeding up (Creating situations of anxiety)
- Unhealthy relationships
- Withdrawal/Isolation
- _____
- _____

Repentance

Prayer

Heavenly Father,

Thank you that I can come before You with full exposure of my sin and You will have healing in Your wings. I repent for partnering with the destructive behaviours I have chosen, knowingly or unknowingly. I repent for hurting myself and others. I renounce each one.

SPEND A FEW MINUTES IN PERSONAL REPENTANCE. RECORD ANY INSIGHTS.

Protective Personalities/Behaviours

THERE EXISTS INTERNAL LIES THAT CERTAIN BEHAVIOURS, SOME DEFENSIVE, some OFFENSIVE, function to maintain your security. However, none of them are helpful or godly. They are not a part of divine character, but that of a false identity or distorted character. They need to be consciously released through prayer.

Once there is an AWARENESS of how the manifestation of this "side of you" is a hindrance, a more intentional choice can be made whether or not to engage in the behaviour. This is a choice of the WILL. An act of the WILL can override EMOTIONS.

Read through the list of common protective personalities/behaviours.[17] Note the ones with which you identify. Add to the list if necessary. Pray to release them. Repeat this process as the layers of healing reveal further personalities/behaviours.

Anger	Invisible	The Perfectionist
Blank	Independence	The Phone
The Bully	The Intimidator	The Pleaser
Confusion	The Martyr	The Protector
Control	Nice	The Rescuer
The Critic	Numb	The Victim
Door Mat	Over Achiever	The Wall
Don't mess with me!	Passive Aggressive	_____
I'm OK		

Release Protective Behaviours

Prayer

Holy Spirit, please show me the traps of the enemy I have fallen into, believing they were a part of my personality; believing they were keeping me or those around me safe. I repent of operating in these behaviours. They are not a part of who You created me to be. I choose to not engage with them any longer. I trust You, Lord Jesus, to keep me and my loved ones safe. I choose not to continually be on the defensive or the offensive. I choose to walk in godly character, demonstrating the fruits of the Spirit. Help me to walk in a manner that is pleasing to You, Lord.

I let go of and cast out _____. (Exhale.)

NOTE ANY REVELATIONS OR INSIGHTS.

STAND IN FREEDOM
Part Four

Kingdom Identity

Kingdom Identity

IN CHRIST, YOU ARE WHO GOD SAYS YOU ARE AS OUTLINED IN THE WORD of God, the Holy Bible. Any beliefs outside this parameter are labels and lies of the enemy—false beliefs creating false identities, robbing you of POWER and AUTHORITY in God's Kingdom, stealing HOPE and JOY, and throwing you into captivity.

You may know your KINGDOM IDENTITY to speak it, but are you fully believing it, fully living it, and walking in its full measure?

When we are walking in the light of God's truth of our identity, godly thought patterns, character, and behaviour is evident.

The Fruit of Kingdom Identity:

Faith	Courage	Generosity
Freedom	Perseverance	Self-Discipline
Hope	Community	Vision
Order	Forgiveness	Self-Control
Truth	Commitment	Excitement
Joy	Purity	Abundance
Blessing	Integrity	Resolve
Goodness	Kindness	Steadfastness
Love	Wisdom	Gentleness
Peace	Patience	Understanding
Power	Faithfulness	Knowledge Of The Lord
Honour	Confidence	Connection
Boldness	Authority	Soft-Heartedness
Fear Of The Lord		

False Identities: Labels and Lies of the enemy

As traumatic events happen in our lives, often when young, the enemy uses that opportune time to plant a lie in our soul (mind, will, emotions) about who we are and who God is. The trauma itself does not have to be "severe" according to our adult standards.

It is the ultimate deception, for the lie may FEEL TRUE, manifesting through our experiences—things that have happened to us, been said to us or about us, or have been done to us.

However, it is not THE TRUTH of God and what He has for us, nor the truth of who we are or who He is. To reiterate, if it does not align with WHO GOD SAYS WE ARE or who Scripture says He is, it is a lie, intent on establishing within you a false identity, sabotaging godly character and behaviour, forcing you to abdicate your power and authority in Christ, and aborting God's plan for your life.

Often the enemy targets his lies on the big picture: our worth, our acceptance, our belonging, our lovability, our healing—all things accomplished with the finished work of the cross.

As the lie is **BELIEVED IN OUR HEARTS** and **AGREED WITH THROUGH OUR WORDS**, a spiritual door is opened. The lie grows, drawing people, events, and circumstances through that open door and into your life in manners that continually reinforce and fortify the lie, expanding its parameters wider and wider, adding layer upon layer of deception, (known as a STRONGHOLD) and eventually producing fruit—rotten fruit. The original lie may even be subconscious, and the instigating trauma may never even be remembered, locked deep within the recesses of your heart.

Demarkations of enemy Traps and Snares:

The rotten fruit of the enemy in your life can include:

Anger	Slander	Fear
Ugliness	Gossip	Anxiety
Fragility	Rudeness	Hopelessness
Lust	Numbness	Grief
Perversion	Boastfulness	Confusion
Frigidity	Unforgiveness	Depression
Doubt	Ungratefulness	Deception
Overwhelm	Pride	Delusion
Sloth	Compromise	Foolishness
Gluttony	Vengeance	Offence
Unbelief	Insecurity	Lack
Shame	Impatience	Limited Authority
Guilt	Abusiveness	Faithlessness
Condemnation	Fear Of Man	Powerlessness
Timidity	Isolation	Complacency
Jealousy	Rebellion	Chaos
Intimidation	Hatred	Accusation
Dullness	Hard-Heartedness	Negativity
Selfish Ambition	Frustration	Despair

STAND IN FREEDOM
Reflective Activity

DO YOU RECOGNIZE ANY OF THIS FRUIT OF THE ENEMY IN YOUR LIFE? HIGHLIGHT ANY THAT YOU FEEL YOU ARE CURRENTLY STRUGGLING WITH.

The Creative Power of Words

CAN BELIEVING A LIE AND SPEAKING IT OVER OURSELVES EITHER ONCE or in endless cycles really have such devastating impact? Let us look at the creative power of words through a Holy Spirit illustration:

> Pour a full glass of juice. That one represents God. Pour a little of the juice from the glass into another glass. That one represents us.
>
> Which one is MORE? (God's glass!)
>
> Which one is SWEETER? (Both the same!!)

This is a clear illustration that the SAME CREATIVE POWER through which God operates—through which He performs miracles, through which He SPOKE the universe into being, through which He creates all things that are, that were, that ever shall be—lives in us.[18]

God has creative power. We have creative power.

The devil's power comes from deception—tricking you into **being in agreement** with his plans and purposes, and professing his lies over your life again and again. In essence, the creative power of your words and the misaligned beliefs of your heart are much of what is keeping you in bondage.

Can you imagine, in those early moments of creation, God's voice thundering across the darkness over the face of the deep ... "LET THERE BE LIGHT!" ... and there was light. "LET US MAKE MAN IN OUR IMAGE ..." so God created man. (GENESIS 1). Now picture that same voice booming ... but the words coming across the expanse are the negative ones we so readily partner with. What words are you speaking over yourselves time and time again?

There is power in the word, and more so when the word and its many nuances are believed and taken into the depths of our heart. But we have a choice. We can use the power of the words we speak over ourselves, over others, to give root to an abundant life. This establishes a foundation of bedrock for a life of limitless victory, and positively influences all those around us. Or, we can choose to use those words to release the deadly poison that will penetrate our own heart and infiltrate those with whom our lives are intertwined. These words bring destruction, decay and death. Death and life are in the power of the tongue (Proverbs 18:21).

The Lord SPOKE creation into existence. What are we speaking into existence with our words?

The Function of Words

WHEN WE HAVE NOT EXPLORED A CONCEPT, WE DON'T REALIZE ITS full depth, its impact, nor its consequences. If it has not been a part of our personal experiences, we may not understand its implications are unfolding all around us; whether we acknowledge its existence or not. What we don't believe, CAN hurt us!

Once we fully understand the impact of words and how they work, we are given the power for change. Let us therefore take a closer look at how they function in the spiritual realm.

We mistakenly think that because words are invisible they are inconsequential—without true power—JUST DISAPPEAR. In reality, we need to think of the spoken word the same as one would conceptualize a relay race, with runners standing ready, waiting for that baton to be passed so they can spring into action. And that action is ABSOLUTELY DEPENDENT on the words being spoken.

As the words come out of our mouths, Holy Spirit and the heavenly hosts are hovering, waiting to put into action any words that align with the words, covenants, laws, and principles of God. As we speak, pray, and declare the Word of God, His promises and His truths about ourselves, we are spiritually strengthened, and God moves on our behalf (Daniel 10:12). This brings us closer and closer to who He has created us to be—our identity. And as we come to understand our identity, we can walk more fully in all that He has called us to do—the fullness of our destiny.

But the spiritual forces of the enemy are also skulking around, running the exact same route with every word that aligns with satan. These are the fiery darts of the wicked one talked about in Ephesians 6, and they can do a lot more damage than a plastic relay baton. These words form the veil that camouflages our identity and thus keeps us from walking in fullness.

All being said, *you are building an army with your words*. Let that concept sink deep into your heart. **YOU ARE BUILDING AN ARMY WITH YOUR WORDS.** Which army do you choose to build?

Not only do words manifest powerfully all around us, they impact our physical bodies. In his book, *"Planting the Heavens,"*[19] Dr. Tim Sheets outlines how the body, right down to the cellular level, submits to what is declared from central command (the brain), and begins to physically produce what is spoken. Hormones that break down the body are also discharged through negative thoughts and words, whereas healing hormones are released with positive ones.

Dr Caroline Leaf also has a book[20] describing this process in depth; providing biological evidence for the biblical Scripture: "For as he thinks in his heart, so is he" (Proverbs 23:7 NKJV), understanding that what you believe in your heart will be expressed out of your mouth.

Repentance

Prayer

Dear Lord, I repent for choosing, knowingly or unknowingly, to agree with enemy lies about my identity rather than choosing to believe I am who You say I am, and that You are who You say You are.

Lord, I am sorry for choosing my feelings over the truth of Your Word, and putting myself, my false beliefs, my wisdom and understanding, over You and Your Word. I repent for not believing You are absolutely good.

Help me know with every ounce of my being that You are who You say You are, and I am who You say I am. This is my Kingdom Identity. Reveal to me any lies and strongholds in my life that are holding me captive—body and soul. Increase my discernment, and grant me wisdom.

I respond to Your call to "Come up higher." Give me eyes to see, ears to hear, and a heart to understand. I want to walk in fullness of relationship with You. I want to walk in the full power and authority You offer me as Your heir, Your child, so I can partner with You in taking back the Kingdom, for Your glory. I want to reconnect with Your design for me, so I can fulfill all the plans You have for my life, to the full measure. I pray this in the precious name of Jesus, Amen.

Untangling the Web of Deceit:
Deciphering Lies

Lies are insidious and malicious. The more deeply rooted, the more impact they can have on us. Many contain that "little bit of truth" which makes them believable, especially as we see the circumstances stemming from them expressed in our lives; however, they warp, twist, and grow, taking on a nasty life of their own.

For example, take the situation, "My mom doesn't love me." This may, in fact, be true. Some people, because of their own woundings, without healing, are incapable of love. But instead of recognizing the problem is with them, not you, this belief can shift into, "If my own mother doesn't love me, who will ever love me?" From this, an unhealthy conclusion is sometimes drawn: "I am therefore unloved." And once this lie takes hold, it can become a full blown identity statement, "I am unlovable …" That is a lie from the pit of hell.

The truth is, God loves you, as stated in His Word. This means, in fact, that it is impossible for you to be "unloved or unloveable," no matter how much you FEEL like this is true. However, as long as you are believing that no one loves you, including God, you will be unwilling to receive (perhaps incapable of receiving) His—or anyone else's love.

You sabotage, isolate and push others far from you. For self protection, you keep your heart COLD and HARD. A cold, hard heart cannot express love nor feel another's love, no matter how much is given. It makes it overwhelming for the people trying to prove their love again and again, not understanding why the person cannot see their love for them. Many eventually walk away with the insatiability of the situation. Thus, what is not God's truth, has become the truth you are living because of your own wounding, beliefs and actions.

I have seen ones who express that no one cares about them, yet personally witnessed people in their lives doing everything they know how to do to express their love for that very person.

Over all, Remember: "NO MATTER WHAT HAS HAPPENED TO YOU, WHAT OTHERS HAVE DONE OR SAID TO YOU, IT DOES NOT MAKE YOU WHO YOU ARE."

Responding

How should we respond when we hear those devious lies whispered into our souls? Do not believe or receive any words that do not align with your Kingdom Identity—who God says you are. Do not accept it into your heart, even if it "feels true" or has been represented in your experiences. CHOOSE instead to believe what God says about you. Know that this is what He has for you and this is where you are going. Understand, however, that perhaps you are not quite there yet—there may need to be some action on your part as you walk out your healing journey.

With any accusations that come against you, internal or external, examine your heart, as David did (Psalm 139). Seek the areas in which there needs to be realignment—areas you are walking in agreement with enemy lies, causing a manifestation of bad fruit in thought, word, or deed. Ask yourself the hard questions—the ones in which you may not wish to hear the honest answers. Be raw, real, and transparent—with yourself, with God, with a prayer partner or minister. Ask for His revelation. Trust that He will give it to you and bring full RESTORATION and HEALING to come out from under the lies and labels and begin to walk in God's truth.

Recognize the SIGNPOSTS that something is wrong. Over-reactions when things do not go your way, physical symptoms, the aforementioned rotten fruits of the enemy manifesting, and telltale emotions are some of the signals that there is a problem. They are like your mind or body screaming out an "SOS" for you to notice that something is wrong—and DO SOMETHING ABOUT IT—not just bury or ignore it! There is usually a HIDDEN lie in which you are in agreement. (As per diagram on page 39. We will be working through this process in Part Five.)

Note the soundtrack in your brain and heart. *"The mind replays what the heart can't delete."* Sometimes your intuition is subtly telling you something is not quite right. You may not know what it is, but it just won't rest.

STAND IN FREEDOM — Reflective Activity

IS THERE A SOUNDTRACK IN YOUR BRAIN OR HEART ON REPEAT?

Dismantling Enemy Labels and Lies

OPENING THE LOCKED DOORS—HIDDEN COMPARTMENTS OF YOUR heart, usually with a sign in bold letters—"DON'T YOU DARE GO THERE!"—and severing enemy partnership and covenants removes his shackles and bondages, cobwebs and dust (Galatians 4:3, Hebrews 2:14-15). This frees up space in your body and soul and increases your CAPACITY to hold and carry the anointing, the joy, the Holy Spirit—all of His fruit. Freedom takes time and comes in layers. You don't have to be "all healed up" before you reap its benefits.

The pathway to dismantling enemy lies and labels over your life is as unique and individual as each person. We need to continually be open to the guidance and direction of Holy Spirit. He will lead us into all truth and revelation (John 16:13). But there are some basic guidelines to give us a starting point.

Think of the process as unravelling a tangled ball of yarn—you find an "END" and start to pull. The ENDS, described as the SOS, are:

- Symptoms of trauma (pg 15, Appendix 1)
- Where trauma is held in your body (pg 33)
- Red Flags/Signposts (pg 37-38)
- Coping mechanisms (g 41)
- Protective behaviours (pg 43)
- Rotten fruit of the enemy manifesting in your life (pg 49)
- Lies you recognize—when you hear them they resonate in your soul (See Appendix 3)

As well, any overreaction can be a signpost in itself. For example, when you have a reaction to a comment, event, or situation that seems significantly stronger than should be warranted in that situation, it is likely you have a previous wounding in that area. Remember, it is similar to poking a physical spot on your body which is already broken or bleeding. You probably would not have even noticed it had it not already been injured.

The current situation is therefore likely NOT the cause of your over-reaction. It would be the trigger, taking you back mentally and emotionally to the original wound (trauma) and the hidden lie that would be attached. That original wound would also have opened a spiritual door, allowing enemy access to deposit his ugly seeds into our soul, which when watered, fester and grow.

Similarly, when fruit of the enemy is displayed in your life, this also indicates an original wounding, often long forgotten, with enemy lies and labels attached. In both of these scenarios, because we believe the lie that comes in at the time of the trauma, we give it life through this belief in our heart and the power of our words as we continue to speak it into our lives —knowingly or unknowingly.

Entangled in with the lie, there will often be a VOW our hearts made in attempt to keep ourselves safe from a reoccurrence of the trauma, but has instead, sealed the deception. Vows sound like, "I will never ..." or "I will always ..." These vows guide our thoughts, mindsets, and behaviours, sometimes consciously, but often through the subconscious mind.

(Review diagram on page 39 if necessary.) "Set your face like flint" and let us now jump into your healing journey with both feet!

STAND IN FREEDOM
Part Five

Connecting with Trauma

faith journey

Connecting with Trauma (Processing Sheet)

Pick an "end" (as noted on page 57) and begin the unraveling process.

Pray to ask Holy Spirit for revelation as to the original trauma identified by the SOS.

What was ORIGINAL TRAUMA?

What did your heart tell you when this happened?

What did you believe?

[This reveals the LIE you believed about God, yourself, or others.]

Repent for partnering with lie, not trusting God, and any ungodly actions on your part.

Come out of alignment with the lie.

Pray for revelation as to the truth of the situation.

"I come out of alignment with the lie that…" "The truth is…"

Was there a vow you made to help you survive? (self-preservation)

"I cancel the vow …"

Is there anyone involved in this situation you need to forgive?

Pray to forgive them. Release all judgments you are holding against others, yourself, and God.

Note:

> Forgiveness does not mean what was done was okay, just or fair.
>
> It does not mean you have to trust or be in relationship.
>
> Forgiveness is giving it over to God, and releasing what you feel was owed to you.
>
> All debts you are holding against others, released.
>
> FORGIVING YOURSELF opens you up to receive His forgiveness.
>
> "FORGIVING GOD" is about releasing judgments against Him.

Cut unholy soul ties with people, places and objects keeping you connected in the spiritual realm.

After David had finished talking with Saul, Jonathon became one in spirit with David, and he loved him as himself.
1 Samuel 18:1

Do you not know that he who unites himself with a prostitute is one with her in body? For it is said, "The two will become one flesh."
1 Corinthians 6:16

… so that even handkerchiefs or aprons that had touched his skin were carried away to the sick, and their diseases left them and evil spirits came out of them.
Acts 19:12

"I break the unholy soul tie with…"

Cut off generational curses.

> …keeping steadfast love for thousands, forgiving iniquity and transgression and sin, but who will by no means clear guilty, visiting the iniquity of the fathers on the children and the children's children, to the third and fourth generation."
> **Exodus 34:7**

"I cut off the generational curse of _____ on my mother's side and my father's side to the fourth generation by the power of the shed blood of Jesus and His sacrificial death on the cross for the sins of mankind."

Cast out evil spirits.
Ask the Holy Spirit for revelation of the names of specific ones.
(See Appendix 4 for the List of spirits and strongmen. This appendix will also help with infilling after deliverance.)

> …they will cast out demons;
> **Mark 16:17**

> The seventy-two returned with joy, saying, "Lord, even the demons are subject to us in your name!"
> **Luke 10:17**

> PAUL … turned and said to the spirit, "I command you in the name of Jesus Christ to come out of her." And it came out that very hour.
> **ACTS 16:18**

"Every spirit of _____, I command you in the name of Jesus Christ to come out now!"

Pray to receive the truth, and record your revelations.

Ask for God's deeper Truth about the whole situation and Invite Jesus into it. What is the whisper of His heart to your soul? [See Appendix 5 for a list of Kingdom Identity Scriptures.]

"Jesus, I invite You into this part of my soul and ask for Your restoration. Show me the truth. Lord, You say that … This is the truth. Put this truth deep into my heart. I invite the truth into my *mind*, my *will* and my *emotions*. This is what I choose to believe. This is what I will align my speech with. I understand feelings will follow. You said it. I believe it. That is all I need."

Is He showing you:

A picture?   A Word?   A Scripture?

Pray for healing and infilling with Holy Spirit.

> When the unclean spirit has gone out of a person, it passes through waterless places seeking rest, but finds none. Then it says, 'I will return to my house from which I are.' And when it comes, it finds the house empty, swept, and put in order. Then it goes and brings with it seven other spirits more evil than itself, and they enter and dwell there, and the last state of the person is worse than the first.
> **Matthew 12:44-45**

Ask the Lord to fill your house!

[See Appendix 3 for a list to help with the infilling of the Spirit.]

"Lord, I ask You to bring restoration to my soul, healing and sealing my wounds. Come fill me with ... (Opposite of the unclean spirits.) Record your revelations.

Pray for restoration. What was lost because of this trauma, its resulting decisions and choices in your life? Record your revelations. Ask the Lord what might need to be done to grieve the loss. This may take time.

… but if he [the thief] is caught,
he will pay sevenfold;
Proverbs 6:31

And the Lord restored the fortunes of Job, when he had prayed for his friends. And the Lord gave Job twice as much as he had before.
Job 42:10

Ask the Lord to reveal any "bad seeds" planted in you and others because of your action/behaviour/choices, or those of others to you. Pray to bring removal of those seeds, that they, like the fig tree Jesus cursed, will shrivel up and die. Ask the Lord for mercy, grace, and blessing over you and the others for what was planted. Record your revelations.

Do not be deceived: God is not mocked, for whatever one sows, that he will also reap.
Galatians 6:7

STAND IN FREEDOM
Part Six

STAYING FREE

Walk in Rest and Peace

INTENTIONALLY MARK THE SABBATH AS A DAY TO REST, FELLOWSHIP, AND participate in enjoyable activities you may not find time for during the week. This is an aspect of rest.

However, walking in rest goes much deeper. It signifies that your HEART IS AT REST and IN PEACE even when the metaphorical storm clouds are brewing around you, or you are caught in the midst of a full-blown tsunami. This state is possible when you have grown your trust in Him in such deep measure that you know that you know that He's got you, He knows everything—you do not, He has a plan for you, it is good—and He is absolutely good.

Practice Gratitude

KNOW THAT AS **PRAISING, REJOICING,** AND GIVING **THANKS** ARE the languages of Heaven in the same way grumbling and complaining are the language of hell.

Find joy in the small things, the simple things; don't wait for the big events or for your circumstances to be as you would wish. Many of our stories are not the way we had envisioned them. The clichéd, "Count your blessings" really can stop the trajectory of the out-of-control spiralling down into the depths of depression and despair.

Focus on Jesus, what you do have, and what is going well in your life. The Bible ensures that we will suffer (1 Peter 5:10). Each of us will have the cross of our story (Luke 14:27), but even that will work together for good:

Not only that, but we rejoice in our sufferings, knowing that suffering produces endurance, and endurance produces character, and character produces hope, and hope does not put us to shame, because God's love has been poured into our hearts through the Holy Spirit who has been given to us.
Romans 5:3-5

Serve

BE THE JONATHON. BE THE ARMOUR BEARER. AS PETER SAYS, HUMBLE yourself and God will lift you up (1 Peter 5:6) … but even then still serve. None of us are too good to clean toilets (Luke 16:12).

Fast

FASTING FROM FOOD—YES, FROM FOOD—KILLS THE FLESH LIKE NOTHING else and forges deep levels of gratitude and Kingdom mindset. Fasting takes you higher and deeper. A shift in our ability and discipline to fast will come when we stop rolling our eyes and confessing, "I hate fasting!" Instead, eagerly put up your hand and squeal in delight, "Pick me, Lord, pick me!" God will give you the grace to fast when He calls you to do so, but that does not mean it will be easy—necessary—but not easy.

Fellowship

Seek a Bible-believing church and attend regularly. Become involved and fellowship with like-minded people—your tribe. Ask the Lord to reveal your tribe to you and call them in if you don't have one. Pray He knits your hearts together.

Live Holy

Be set apart and consecrate yourself: Be vigilant as to what you put into your eye gates and ear gates.

You cannot drink the cup of the Lord and the cup of demons too; you cannot have a part in both the Lord's table and the table of demons.
1 Corinthians 10:21

Consecrate yourselves, for tomorrow the Lord will do wonders among you.
Joshua 3:5

Obedience and Surrender

Cultivate an obedient, surrendered lifestyle. Surrender both your WILL and your AGENDA. Your *will* is tied to the bigger overall picture of the dreams and visions you have for your life, and the life decisions you make according to your judgements and values based on these dreams and visions for your life. Your *agenda* is in reference to the smaller, daily choices. Ensure they are in alignment with the Father's will for your life. Be obedient in both. Obedience is KEY.

"Not everyone who says to me, "Lord, Lord,' will enter the kingdom of heaven, but the one who does the will of my Father who is in heaven.
Matthew 7:21

During the days of Jesus' life on earth, he offered up prayers and petitions with fervent cries and tears to the one who could save him from death, and he was heard because of his reverent submission. Son though he was, he learned obedience from what he suffered and, once made perfect, he became the source of eternal salvation for all who obey him.
Hebrews 5:7-9 NIV

If Jesus had to submit and obey, how much more so should we. Give God your "yes." You never know where it will lead! What an adventure!

Keep seeking your Healing

Healing comes in stages and layers. Do not give up. Keep noticing what you notice, connecting the dots, and allowing the Holy Spirit to continue to lead you on your journey to fullness and freedom. If it is not good, it is not DONE!

Be the Gold Refined in the Fire

Much insight as to what the Lord requires of us is given in Revelation chapters 2 and 3. Revelation 2 reminds us, "Whoever has ears let him hear what the spirit says to the churches."

He commends the churches for their:

Deeds	Faith	Hard Work	Repentance
Love	Service	Perseverance	

He honours them for:

Not tolerating wicked people

Their faithfulness

Not being afraid of suffering

Keeping His command to endure patiently

Being faithful even to the point of death

Being earnest

Accepting the rebuke and discipline of the Lord

Enduring hardships for His Name

He reminds them:

Do all the Lord puts in front of you—and finish!

Wake up! Strengthen what remains and is about to die, for I have found your deeds unfinished in the sight of my God.
Revelation 3:2

STAND IN FREEDOM
Reflective Activity

WHERE ARE YOU ALONG THE PATH TO STAYING FREE? WHAT CAN YOU IMPLEMENT TO HELP YOU?

Endnotes

1. van der Kolk, Bessel. *The Body Keeps the Score: Brain, Mind, and Body in the Healing of Trauma.* New York: Penguin Books, 2015, pg 66.
2. van der Kolk, Bessel. *The Body Keeps the Score: Brain, Mind, and Body in the Healing of Trauma.* New York: Penguin Books, 2015, pg 53.
3. Levine, Peter. *Waking the Tiger: Healing Trauma.* Berkeley: North Atlantic Books, 1997, pg 20.
4. Levine, Peter. *Waking the Tiger: Healing Trauma.* Berkeley: North Atlantic Books, 1997, pg 19, 24, 43, 45, 53, 54, 59.
5. Levine, Peter. *Waking the Tiger: Healing Trauma.* Berkeley: North Atlantic Books, 1997, pg 54.
6. Levine, Peter. *Waking the Tiger: Healing Trauma.* Berkeley: North Atlantic Books, 1997, pg 63.
7. Levine, Peter. *Waking the Tiger: Healing Trauma.* Berkeley: North Atlantic Books, 1997, pg 168.
8. van der Kolk, Bessel. *The Body Keeps the Score: Brain, Mind, and Body in the Healing of Trauma.* New York: Penguin Books, 2015, pg 3.
9. Levine, Peter. *Waking the Tiger: Healing Trauma.* Berkeley: North Atlantic Books, 1997, pg 219.
10. van der Kolk, Bessel. *The Body Keeps the Score: Brain, Mind, and Body in the Healing of Trauma.* New York: Penguin Books, 2015, pg 213.
11. van der Kolk, Bessel. *The Body Keeps the Score: Brain, Mind, and Body in the Healing of Trauma.* New York: Penguin Books, 2015, Pg 55.
12. Levine, Peter. *Waking the Tiger: Healing Trauma.* Berkeley: North Atlantic Books, 1997, pg 41,107, 147-149, 162, 165
13. Ferris, Clem. *Stewarding Prophecy: Waging Warfare With God's Word.* June 18, 2020, page 58.
14. Lee, Witness. 2014. "Dealing with Our Inward Parts for the Growth in Life." Living Stream Ministry. http://www.ministrysamples.org/excerpts/THE-SOUL-HAVING-THREE-PARTS.HTML. (Accessed June 25, 2024)
15. *The Human Spirit*, June 22, 2015. "The 3 parts of Man — Spirit, Soul, Body." Bibles for America. https://blog.biblesforamerica.org/the-three-parts-of-man-spirit-soul-and-body. (Accessed June 25, 2024).
16. Souza, Katie. *Matter Holds Memory: Where Trauma is Stored in Your Body.* Youtube, December 20, 2023. (Accessed July 17th, 2024)
17. Dye, Michael. *The Genesis Process.* https://www.genesisprocess.org (accessed June 25, 2024).
18. Sikalangwe, Alinani. Holy Spirit-led illustration at #ALightHouse, 2023.
19. Sheets, Tim. *Planting the Heavens.* Shippensburg: Destiny Image, *2017.*
20. Leaf, Caroline. *Switch on Your Brain: The Key to Peak Happiness, Thinking, and Health.* Ada: Baker Books, 2015.

*Please note: I do not agree with everything in Lenine's and van der Kolk's books; however, they have a deep understanding of the physiology of trauma, which can be applied.

STAND IN FREEDOM
Appendices

Appendix 1 -
Symptoms of Trauma

Appendix 2 -
Case Studies

Appendix 3 -
Enemy Lies, Spirit Families and Holy Spirit Infilling

Appendix 4 -
Biblical Strongmen

Appendix 5 -
Kingdom Identity Scriptures

Appendix 1- Symptoms of Trauma

Symptoms of Trauma[12]

Flashbacks
Anxiety
Panic attacks
Depression
Feelings of impending doom
Feelings of detachment
Alienation
Isolation
Diminished interest in life
Psychotic complaints
Lack of openness
Violent unprovoked rage attacks
Repetitive destructive behaviours
Anorexia
Insomnia
Promiscuity
Phobias
Mental blankness (numb)
Avoidance behaviour
Amnesia
Forgetfulness
Inability to love, nurture or bond
Low physical energy
Immune system problems
Endocrine problems (thyroid)
Asthma
Digestive issues
Neck problems/pain
Back problems/pain
Blindess
Deafness
Paralysis in legs, arms

Manic hyperactivity
Hyper-arousal
Dissociation
Helplessness (Victim mentality)
Hypervigilance
Intrusive imagery
Extreme sensitivity to light or sound
Exaggerated emotional and startle responses
Nightmares
Night terrors
Abrupt mood swings
Rage reactions
Temper tantrums
Shame
Reduced ability to deal with stress
Difficulty sleeping
Attraction to dangerous situations
Frequent crying
Exaggerated or diminished sexual activity
Fear of dying, going crazy or having shortened life
Reduced ability to deal with stress or make plans
Excessive shyness
Muted or diminished emotional responses
Inability to make commitments
Chronic fatigue
Headaches/migraines
Premenstrual syndrome
Difficulty in participating in new situations
Spastic colon
Bronchitis
Gastro intestinal problems

Appendix 2 - Case Studies

Case Study 1 - Male child - 2.5 years old

Behaviour:
Bites, pushes, refuses to take naps, constant crying, head banging, rocking
Does not feel safe with any staff member at his daycare
Fluctuates between despondent collapse and angry defiance

Observations:
Clings to his mother, hiding his face - she responds, "Don't be such a baby."
He startles when a door is banged down the hallway, burrows deep in his mother's lap
Mother pushes him away; he responds by sitting in a corner and banging his head
Mother responds by remarking: "He does that to bug me."

Diagnosis:
Depression, ADHD, Oppositional Defiance Disorder, Intermittent Explosive Disorder

1. Do the labels of his diagnosis accurately depict/explain the behaviour of this child?
2. Will any of these diagnoses help in the healing processes for this child?

Mother's background:
Mother had been abandoned by parents, raised by relatives who hit her, ignored her, sexually abused her at 13 years old
Child's father was drunken boyfriend who left with news of pregnancy
Mother remarks child is "Just like his father—good for nothing." Mother has had numerous violent relationships, but was sure "It was too late at night for him to notice."

3. How does adding the mother's background help with understanding his behaviour?
4. What would you determine was the underlying cause of his behaviours?
5. How would you help with the healing process of this child?

Case Study 2 - Female Teenager - 13 years old

Observations/Behaviours:
Isolates, controlling, explosive, sexualized, intrusive, vindictive, and narcissistic. Seductive with any male who crossed her path

Diagnosis:
Bipolar Disorder, Intermittent Explosive Disorder, Reactive Attachment Disorder, ADD, Hyperactive Disorder, Oppositional Defiance Disorder, Substance Abuse disorder

1. Do the labels of her diagnosis accurately depict/explain the behaviour of this child?
2. Will any of these diagnoses help in the healing processes for this child?

Background:
Taken away from biological mom because of drug abuse
First adoptive mom fell ill and died, moved from foster home to foster home before being adopted again. Was abused sexually and physically by various boyfriends and temporary caregivers. Hospitalized numerous times for suicide attempts. She describes herself as disgusting and says she wishes she were dead.

3. How does adding the child's background help with understanding the behaviour?
4. What would you determine was the underlying cause of her behaviours?
5. How would you help with the healing process of this child?

*Case Studies adapted from van Der Kolk's *The Body Keeps the Score* - pg 152-153

Appendix 3 - Enemy Lies, Spirit Families, and Holy Spirit Infilling

The enemy is not the creative genius the Lord is! He uses the same tactics time and again. And he will continue to use them ON YOU—the same ones, over and over again—until they stop working ON YOU. Though some lies are unique to individuals, many fit into a common playbook that has spanned the ages.

This is a tool, a reference, a starting point. It is by no means complete! Trust the Lord to reveal what you need to know, when you need to know it! (1 Corinthians 2:10, John 14:26, John 16:13)

[Note: You may be either the receiver … or the giver of these statements, to yourself or others. It indicates you are operating under the influence of this spirit.]

SPIRIT FAMILY:
DISAPPOINTMENT/DISCOURAGEMENT/DESPAIR/HOPELESSNESS/DESPONDENCY/APATHY/GRIEF/DEPRESSION/VICTIM MENTALITY/DULLNESS

Nothing I do matters.
Nothing ever works.
I don't make a difference.
That's the story of my life.
    (In response to negative events)
Opportunities are always stolen from me.
I'm just going to be disappointed again.
Nothing is working.
It will never work.
I can't catch a break.
Nothing will ever change.

There is no point.
Here it goes again.
I will never measure up.
I will just fail again.
I am a failure.
I don't measure up.
I will never measure up.
This is just the way it is.
That's life.
That's just the way life is.

I am not capable.
I'm not good at anything.
That's too big for me.
I am hopeless.
It is hopeless.

Things never go my way.
It is happening again.
Things don't work out for me.
I'm stuck.
I have worked hard all my life and have nothing to show for it.

> Fill with: hope, encouragement, energy, enthusiasm, eagerness, excitement, joy, God-confidence, promise, wisdom.

Spirit Family:

REJECTION/ABANDONMENT/BETRAYAL/PERFORMANCE ORIENTATION/SHAME/GUILT/ CONDEMNATION/BLAME/ORPHAN SPIRIT/DEPENDENCE/CO-DEPENDENCE/OBSESSION

God, why didn't you ...
No one loves me.
No one cares about me.
God does not care about me.
God does not love me.
I am unloved.
I am unloveable.
I will never be accepted.
I am not enough.
I am not good enough.
I will always be alone.
I am not worthy of love.
I am not worth it.
I am not worthy.
I am not worthy of anything good.
Who would do that for me?
I am insignificant.

Who would invest in me?
Who would want to be with me?
I am unnoticed.
No one sees me.
People I like will never like me.
I am not worth pursuing.
I am invisible.
I am less than.
I am forgotten.
God has forgotten me.
I am unchosen.
I am uninvited.
No one ever invites me.
I am always overlooked.
I am unimportant.
I do not matter.

What I do is insignificant.
I don't want to offend anyone.
I don't want to disappoint anyone.
How could you have done that.
God can't love you anymore.
You will never be forgiven.
You are too bad to be forgiven.
You are too bad to be loved/accepted.
Why would someone want to be friends with me?
Why would someone want to spend time with me?
I'd rather be in a bad relationship than no relationship at all.
I could fall off the face of the earth and no one would notice.

I have no voice.
No one hears me.
I have nothing to say.
Look at you.
I am broken.
I am inferior.
I am inadequate.
I don't want to hurt anyone.

Fill with: acceptance, love, faithfulness, belonging, trust, peace, worthiness in Christ, restoration, redemption, freedom.

Spirit Family:

DEATH/DEVOURER/DESTRUCTION/MURDER/SUICIDE/INFIRMITY/SELF HARM/POVERTY

They would be better off without me.
I will always be hurt.
I will always feel like this.
I wish I was dead.
I'm done.
I wish this was over.
I can't do this anymore.
I'll never make it.
I can't stop eating.
I am jinxed.
My body is deteriorating with age.

Get your head out of the clouds.
I receive the opposite of what I ask for.
I will never have what I truly want.
I have _____ (illness/disease).
My _____ (illness/disease) …
I will never be truly free.
I will never live in peace and joy.
I will never be better.
I will always be broken.
Nothing goes right for me.

My eyes are getting worse as I age.
I always get the short end of the stick.
I need something sweet after I eat a meal.
I deserve what happens to me.
Things start out well but always deteriorate/go bad.

I can't stop smoking.
How come I can't stop eating?
Everything gets taken from me.
I'm going to kill you.

> Fill with: life, new birth, creativity, health, abundance, love, inspiration, protection, grace, favour.

Spirit Family:
Unbelief/mistrust/doubt/confusion/chaos/mental illness

If only that were true.
I can't trust God.
God lies.
That will never happen.
That is impossible.
People say they are going to but they don't.
I don't feel that is true.
God doesn't keep His promises.
God is punishing me.
I feel …
I need change. (For the sake of change, not necessarily for the better.)

Stop dreaming.
I'm confused.
I have no purpose.
I am terrible with names.
My memory is bad.
My needs will not be met.
I have the worst timing.
I am who I feel I am.

> Fill with: faith, inspiration, clarity of mind, peace, order, tenacity, hope, belief perseverance, God strategies, trust.

SPIRIT FAMILY:

ANGER/RAGE/INTIMIDATION/UNFORGIVENESS/CONTROL/MANIPULATION/NARCISSISM/ BITTERNESS/VENGEANCE/SELF-HATRED/HATRED/DISGUST/ARROGANCE/SECRECY/LYING SPIRIT

He/She made me so mad.
Who do you think you are?
Look what you made me do.
After all I have done for you!
I hate myself.
I hate my life.
I hate my family.
I hate you.
I hate my body (body part.)
If you really loved me ...
If you don't ...

You are making a big deal about nothing.
It's not that bad.
You are going to pay.
Look at you/him/her.
You disgust me.
You'll be sorry.
Don't tell.
If I/you say something ...
Be quiet.
Don't tell.
Shut up!

Fill with: peace, forgiveness, love, trust, healing, wholeness, courage, empathy, respectfulness, humility, gentleness, sincerity, integrity, self-discipline.

SPIRIT FAMILY:

ACCUSATION/SLANDER/GOSSIP/CHARACTER ASSASSINATION/MALICE/IMPATIENCE

How could you?
You will always be ...
You are just like ...

Fill with: humility, truth, compassion, patience, kindness.

Spirit Family:
disobedience/rebellion/jealousy/envy/pride/stubbornness/insatiability/greed/idolatry/selfish ambition/independence

What is the point?
Why should I?
What have they ever done for me?
How come they get to …
They get all the breaks.
It's not fair.

What if I don't have enough?
I just need a little more.
I can take care of myself.
I'm better off alone.
Why can't I …
I have to do everything myself.

> Fill with: obedience, soft-heartedness, fear of the Lord, intimacy, fulfillment, humility, charity, generosity, thanksgiving, unity, righteousness, empathy, reverence.

Spirit Family:
fear/timidity/terror/shock/trauma/anxiety

My anxiety …
I have anxiety …
I will never do that again.
God can't be trusted.
I am shy.
I can't do it.
I can't …

I could never do that.
I won't have enough.
I am not safe.
God can't keep me safe.
God can't keep my family safe.
The enemy is more powerful than God.
The enemy is bigger than God.

> Fill with: peace, courage, healing, boldness. Pray for a restoration of the body to its original design, cells vibrating at their God-given frequency, removal of all shock, terror, trauma, removal of all memory in the cells of traumatic event.

SPIRIT FAMILY:
LUST/PERVERSION/JEZEBEL/PROFANITY/OBSCENITY/ADDICTION/INSATIABLE

Everyone is doing it.
I am human.
I have needs.
Why not? What does it hurt?
It is a victimless crime.
It is not hurting anyone.
I can't help it.
Just this once.

I have to.
No one has to know.
I can't handle things without it.
One more time.
I can handle it.
It calms me down.
It relaxes me.
It is never enough.

Fill with: purity, satisfaction, fullness, wholeness, self-control.

SPIRIT FAMILY OF SELF-PRESERVATION:

These spirits influence your personality. They are not a part of who you were designed to be. Cast them out.

anger, criticism, tough, intimidation, bully, control, aggressive, demanding, abuse, blank, shutdown, numb, callousness, wall, isolation, walked on, invisible, shy, silence numb, confusion, justification, rationalization, phony, nicety, independence, martyr, perfectionism, overachiever, pleaser, rescuer, protector, needy, victim, passive aggressive, busyness, over-indulgence

Appendix 4 - Spiritual Strongmen

Spirit of Divination
Manifestations:
Fortuneteller, soothsayer, warlock, satanist, satanic ritual abuse, witch, Wiccan, druid, pagan, stargazer, zodiac, horoscopes, palm readers, tarot cards, ouija boards, rebellion, hypnotist, enchanter, drugs, *pharmakos*, water witching, sorcerers, divination, magic, python spirit, Jezebel spirit

Loose: The Holy Spirit and Gifts

Familiar Spirit
Manifestations:
Ancestors, control, witchcraft, ouija, juju, satanism, divination, witches, necromancer, medium, peeping, muttering, yoga, clairvoyant, spiritist, drugs, *pharmakos*, passive mind-dreamers, false prophecy, mediums, spells, curses, hexes, potions, dust, chants, incantations, sacrifices, offerings, occult, covenant vows, python, demon smells, various incense, sounds and beats, horoscope, New Age, psychic abilities, eastern religions

Loose: The Holy Spirit and Gifts

Familiar Spirit of Jealousy
Manifestations:
Control, envy, hatred, bitterness, anger, rage, un-forgiveness, vengefulness violence, murder, profanity, arthritis, bone conditions, competition, contention, cruelty, division, fighting, quarrelling, restlessness, revenge, selfishness, spite, suspicion, wrath, conceited provoking, controlled by own desires, strife, evil sensuality, selfish ambition, covertness, carnality

Loose: The love of God

Lying Spirit
Manifestations:
Strong deceptions, flattery, superstitions, religious bondages, false prophecy, accusations, slander, gossip, lies, false teachers, guile, exaggeration, falsehood, false doctrine, false religion, craftiness, superstition, hypocrisy, self-deception, adultery, fornication, sodomy, criticism, mystification, deviation, esteems self high, homosexuality, insinuation, isolation, profanity, "I love you," vain imaginations, vain notions, vanity, denies deity of Jesus, cannot stand the truth

Loose: The Spirit of truth, who is Jesus

Perverse Spirit
Manifestations:
Broken spirit, evil actions, atheism, abortion, child abuse, filthy mind, doctrinal error, sexual perversions, sexual immorality, twisting the Word, Foolish, chronic worrier, contentions, incest, pornography, fornication, adultery, prostitution, lust, hate, hatred of God, homosexuality, perversion of Gospel, rebellion, self-lovers, wounds spirit, wrong teaching

Loose: Holy Spirit, pureness, holiness

Spirit of Haughtiness
Manifestations:
Arrogance, smugness, pride, idleness, scornful, strife, obstinate, stubbornness, self-deception, contentious, self-righteousness, rebellion, rejection of God, brashness, refusal to listen, Jezebel, gossip, controlling spirit, egotistic, haughtiness, mockery, pretentious, vanity, wrathful

Loose: humble and contrite spirit

Spirit of Heaviness
Manifestations:
Excessive mourning, sorrow, sadness, grief, insomnia, self-pity, rejection, broken-heart, despair, dejection, hopelessness, depression, suicidal thoughts, inner hurts, torn spirit, heaviness, oppression, fatigue, exhaustion, paranoia, mental illness, gluttony, devil is god, discouragement, fear, gloominess, idolatry, loneliness, troubled spirit

Loose: The comforter, Oil of joy, Garment of praise

Spirit of Whoredom
Manifestations:
Unfaithfulness, adultery, fornication, spirit/soul/body prostitution, chronic dissatisfaction, love of money, idolatry, excessive appetite, love of food, controlling spirit that competes with God, ambition in workplace, put others down, excessive cosmetic surgery, love of possessions and corruption, love of the world, self-worship, selfish compromise, physical looks valued over character, all sexual sin emotionally weak, homosexuality, pornography, unclean spirit, unequally yoked, worldly lifestyle

Loose: Spirit of God, Pure Spirit, Holiness, Commitment, Insatiable Ever Increasing Hunger for more of God and His Presence

Deaf and Dumb Spirit
Manifestations:
Dumbness, mute, deafness, dyslexia, learning difficulties, crying, drowning, tearing, wallowing, blindness, mental illness, inner ear problems, suicidal tendencies, lunacy, madness, insanity, bruising, foaming at the mouth, seizures, epilepsy, burns, gnashing of teeth, pining away, prostration, fits, convulsions, speech loss, stuttering, eye diseases, motionless stupors, schizophrenia

Loose: Resurrection Life and Gifts of Healings

Spirit of Bondage
Manifestations:
Fears, addictions, fear of death, captivity to satan, servant of corruption, compulsive sin, bondage to sin, domination, manipulation, OCD, all forms of 'religion,' cult and mind control, bullying in relationships, corrupted belief system, abuse, bruised, broken, ambition, anguish of spirit, bitterness, spiritual blindness, cancer, greed, lust, love of money, over-eating, destructive power, satanic activity, un-forgiveness, occult practices, demonic dreams, nightmares, self-harm, suicide, premature death

Loose: Liberty, Spirit of Adoption

Spirit of Fear
Manifestations:
Fears, phobias, heart attacks, torment, horror, fear of man, nightmares, terrors, anxiety, stress, tension, fear of death, untrusting, doubt, eating disorders, insomnia, compulsive behaviours, anguish, worry, inadequacy, inferiority, timidity

Loose: Love, Power, and a Sound Mind; Perfect Love casts out all fear

Seducing Spirits
Manifestations:
Hypocritical lies, seared conscience, evil conscience, attractions to false prophets and lying signs and wonders, deception, wandering from Truth, fascination with evil ways/persons/objects, seducers, enticers, erroneous teaching, rejects truth of God's Word, idolater, leads people into error, believes doctrines of demons, unbelief in the ways of God, hellish doctrines

Loose: Holy Spirit of Truth

Spirit of Anti-Christ
Manifestations:
Denies Deity of Christ, denies atonement, against Christ and His teaching, humanism, worldly speech and actions, teachers of heresy, anti-Christian, deceiver, lawlessness, from Babylon, cults, creeds, rejects Jesus and Holy Spirit, offers false doctrine, false religion, secularism, atheism, attempts Christ's place, blasphemes, controlling spirit, legalism, New Age, opposes man of God, persecutes saints, speaks against the gifts of God, Substitutes the Blood, suppresses ministries, worldly speech and actions

Loose: Spirit of Truth

Spirit of Error
Manifestations:
Error, un-submissive, false doctrines, false teachers, false prophets, unteachable, servant of corruption contentions, defensive, argumentative, New Age, covetousness, damnation, defilement, discouragement, discontentment, doubt, defeat, deceptive words, lust of the flesh, lust of the eyes, pride of life, stubbornness, unholy spirits, wrong companions, wrong counsel

Loose: Spirit of Truth

Spirit of Poverty and Lack
Manifestations:
Related to greed and fear of loss, not necessarily wealth, laziness, greed, looting, stealing, concealing sin, lack of generosity, belief in poverty, covetousness, debt, dishonesty, hate of rich people, idolatry of possessions, not believing in covenant blessings, stealing, refusing to pay others for their labour, robbing God by not giving

Loose: Inheritance and blessing, Spirit of generosity,
What defeats it: looking to the true source, giving to the Lord, giving to the poor, hard work, generosity, obedience to the Word of God

Spirit of Death
Manifestations:
Suicide attempts, believes lie to kill oneself, lost faith in God, thoughts of destruction and hopelessness, curse of death, certain infirmities, victimization, abusive, violent situations, self-harm, near death accidents, unwanted pregnancies, attempted miscarriages, contemplated abortion, word curses of premature death, rejection of the unborn child, abandonment, depression through upheaval of broken relationship, constant talk about dying, death wish, low self-esteem, forced bad-eating habits, self-hatred, drug abuse, alcoholism, despair, mental disorders (Bipolar, Schizophrenia, Clinical Depression, Borderline Personality Disorder),

Loose: Spirit of life, love, joy, and peace in the Holy Spirit

Spirit of Infirmity
Manifestations:
Sickness, suffering, cancer, all diseases, disabilities, pain, terminal illness, bent body/spine, impotence, frail, lame, asthma, hay fever, allergies, arthritis, weakness, lingering disorders, oppression, colds, eyes/ear problems, hunchback, lung issues, muscles issues, frail heart, sinuses, viruses

Loose: Spirit of Life and Gifts of Healing

Source and for more Information, including Scripture references:
Robeson, Gerry & Carol. *Strongman's His Name, What's His Game?* New Kensington: Whitaker House, 2000.

Buttner, Len, "Seventeen Strongholds and Their Manifestations," Eagleascend, April 2016, eagleascend.com. (Accessed June 2024)

Appendix 5 - Our Kingdom Identity in Christ

We are holy and faithful - Colossians 1:2
Redeemed in Him - Colossians 1:14
He holds all things together - Colossians 1:17
We have our hope of glory in Him - Colossians 1:27
We are rooted and built up - Colossians 2:7
In Him the whole fullness of deity dwells bodily - Colossians 2:9
Complete/Filled in Him - Colossians 2:10
We come into reality - Colossians 2:17
Raised with Christ, hidden with Christ in God - Colossians 3:1-3
Our life is now hidden with Christ in God - Colossians 3:3
Chosen to be the holy people God loves - Colossians 3:12
We have wisdom from God - 1 Corinthians 1:30
God's temple - 1 Corinthians 3:17
I belong to Christ - 1 Corinthians 3:23
A temple of the Holy Spirit - 1 Corinthians 6:19-20
Bought with a price - 1 Corinthians 6:20
The body of Christ - 1 Corinthians 12:27
Our labor is not in vain - 1 Corinthians 15:58
A new creation with a new life - 2 Corinthians 5:17
Reconciled to God - 2 Corinthians 5:18
Christ's ambassador - 2 Corinthians 5:20
Made right with God through Christ - 2 Corinthians 5:21
Blessed with every spiritual blessing - Ephesians 1:3
Holy and without fault in His eyes in Christ - Ephesians 1:4
Adopted to sonship - Ephesians 1:5
Accepted, belonging to Christ - Ephesians 1:6
Free, redeemed and forgiven - Ephesians 1:7
United with Christ, receiving an inheritance/Chosen - Ephesians 1:11
We are for the praise of his glory - Ephesians 1:12
Loved, given life, saved - Ephesians 2:4-5
We have been seated in the heavenly realms - Ephesians 2:6
We've been given the incomparable riches of God's grace - Eph. 2:7
Saved through faith - Ephesians 2:8
God's masterpiece/handiwork, created to do good works - Eph. 2:10
Near to God through Jesus' blood - Ephesians 2:13
We are built together as a holy building - Ephesians 2:22
We may approach God boldly and confidently - Ephesians 3:12
Rooted in love - Ephesians 3:17

We are light - Ephesians 5:8
Deeply loved - Ephesians 3:17-18
Nourished, cherished - Ephesians 5:29
Member of Christ's Body, the church - Ephesians 5:29
Crucified with Christ - Galatians 2:20
We become God's children - Galatians 3:26
Clothed with Christ, all one in Christ Jesus - Galatians 3:27-28
Filled with the fruit of the spirit - Galatians 5:22
Created in the image of God- Genesis 1:27
Engraved on the palm of God's hand - Isaiah 49:16
Anointed - Isaiah 61:1
Known, set apart - Jeremiah 1:5
A child of God - John 1:12
A friend of Jesus - John 15:15
Chosen and appointed to bear lasting fruit - John 15:16
The salt of the earth - Matthew 5:13
The light of the world - Matthew 5:14
Called to maturity - Matthew 5:48
We are overcomers - John 5:45
A chosen people, a royal priesthood, a holy nation, God's own possession, that you may declare the praises of him who called you out of darkness into his wonderful light. - 1 Peter 2:9
Chosen - 1 Peter 2:9
Healed, dead to sin - 1 Peter 2:24
Uniquely gifted - 1 Peter 4:10
All our needs are met according to his glorious riches - Philippians 4:19
The people of God, the sheep of His pasture - Psalm 100:3
Seen by God - Psalm 139:7-10
Fearfully and wonderfully made Psalm 139:14
Beloved by God - Romans 1:7
Called to be a saint - Romans 1:7
Grace-filled - Romans 5:17
No longer slaves to sin - Romans 6:6
Alive in Christ - Romans 6:11
There is no condemnation for us in Christ - Romans 8:1
Set free - Romans 8:2
Heir of God - Romans 8:17
Called according to His purposes - Romans 8:28
Conformed to the image of Jesus - Romans 8:29
More than conquerors -Romans 8:37

We can never be separated from God's love - Romans 8:39
We who are many form one body - Romans 12:5
We have different gifts to use in service to the body of Christ - Ro 12:6-8
Rescued - 1 Thessalonians 1:10
We will rise from the dead - 1 Thessalonians 4:16
We can give thanks in all circumstances - 1 Thessalonians 5:18
We have faith, hope, and love - 1Timothy 1:1, 14
We have the promise of life - 2 Timothy 1:1
Citizens of heaven -Philippians 3:20
The head and not the tail; above and not below - Deuteronomy 28:13
We have a spirit of love, power, and self-control - 2 Timothy 1:7
We have authority - Mark 16:17, Luke 10:19, Matthew 10:8
We are victorious; we have the victory - 1 Corinthians 15:57
We are armed - 2 Corinthians 10:4-5

STAND IN FREEDOM
Notes